T0197460

HOW TO LOVE

WISDOM OF THE AGES

IN A

COUPLE OF PAGES

ANTHONY WEBSTER

Copyright © 2010 by Anthony Webster. 565326

All rights reserved. No part of this book may
be reproduced or transmitted in any form or by
any means, electronic or mechanical, including
photocopying, recording, or by any information storage
and retrieval system, without permission in writing from
the copyright owner.

To order additional copies of this book, contact:
Xlibris
844-714-8691
www.Xlibris.com
Orders@Xlibris.com

ISBN: 978-1-4500-0939-3 (sc)
ISBN: 979-8-3694-1095-0 (e)

Print information available on the last page

Rev. date: 11/06/2023

IDEALS AND PRINCIPLES
FOR PEACEFUL AND
HARMONIOUS LIVING

"If the people be led by laws, and uniformity sought to be given them by punishments, they will try to avoid the punishment, but have no sense of shame. If they be led by virtue, and conformity sought to be given them by the rules of propriety, they will have the sense of shame, and moreover will become good".

Confucius

ACKNOWLEDGEMENTS

I want to express my sincere gratitude to Ramon Fuller of Starplus Communications for the dedication, expertise and great ideas he contributed in bringing this work to fruition. This book would never have been written were it not for my grandmother Theresa Louisa Chinapoo, who would forever remain my most unforgettable character because of her wisdom, wit and self empowerment in an age when the expression was not even used. When wishing to firmly establish her authority, she would say with all the verve and gusto she could muster, " I am Theresa Louisa Chinapoo and when I talk, no dog bark!" To her, love also meant intervention and affirmative action. She rescued me from my very young and inexperienced mother when at the age of three months I contracted pneumonia. She kept me, and with the help of my aunt Theresa Fuller brought me up as their own child, loved me and taught me how to love and live constructively, mainly by example and the use of short phrases similar to those contained in this work. Throughout my life I profited from these teachings and realized that this was a tried and tested means of communicating effectively, seeing that it had worked for me. I remain forever grateful to her, God bless her wonderful soul.

Anthony Webster

A WORD FROM THE AUTHOR

A quick perusal of this book may turn you off. At first glance it may seem to you to be just a list of instructions about all the things we already know we should be doing to achieve some measure of order, stability and peace. So what else is new?

While most of us know these things, some of us may need to be reminded. And unfortunately the ones who need to be reminded may not be the ones who would be attracted to buy or read this book. Some of these same people may say, " How to Love? I know how to love already".

So, you will ask, why write a book for people who don't think they will need it? Good question. That's where you come in. The universe supplies us with all our needs. The fact that you were attracted to this book means something. Probably you have a problem in your home, your school or the office. Probably you have a role to play in bringing happiness to the lives of others, who haven't got a clue how to do it.

Life is about the pursuit of happiness, not simply about the following of a set of rules. The rules are supposed to help us to help ourselves achieve this happiness.

Please don't let the 'rules' get you down. While it may put a lot of the onus on you, because of the knowledge you have, remember its purpose. As the words of an old song goes:

> I want to live until I die,
> I want to laugh, not gonna cry,
> Until my numbers up,
> I'm gonna fill my cup,
> I'm gonna live, live, live until I die.

These ideals and principles should serve as reminders to you and those around you to live a happier life, by reminding people to observe some simple rules of gracious and constructive living, while you go ahead with the business and enjoyment of living. I have the "Ideals and Principles of Peaceful and Harmonious Living at Home" stuck up on my refrigerator at home. I have the "Office" one stuck up in my office. I know they help. Try it. Enjoy your life.

CONTENTS

PROLOGUE

The first name that came to me for this book was 'THINGS WE DON'T TALK ENOUGH ABOUT and should do' and as you see I changed to this slightly controversial title 'How to Love'. But if you think about it, you will eventually agree that it does make a lot of sense.

Perhaps I should explain. *Saying* that you love is one thing, *showing* how you love is another. Sometimes we say one thing and do something else. So to prove that we mean what we say we must behave in a manner consistent with our words. We love by showing, in all the small ways, respect and consideration for others. **The pursuit of a virtuous life is the answer to peaceful and harmonious living.** These short, simple and familiar maxims are topics for discussion, especially in the home where some parents feel embarrassed or reluctant to talk to their children about these matters, and in the schools where virtuous living is considered the private domain of each child. Everyday we see the outcome of such an approach—indiscipline, intolerance and violence. *Learning how to live harmoniously and peacefully with others must also be taught and learnt.*

Parents/Teachers:

Pick a topic and discuss one everyday with your children/pupils. Make a point of discussing the virtues, it helps in character building and gives people ideals to aspire to, such as patience, humility, fortitude, honesty, abstention, contentment, courage, kindness and discretion.

Discuss the vices which people are prone to and make them aware of the pitfalls of threading these paths such as laziness, envy, pride, quarrelsomeness, making confusion, overindulgence, drugs, drunkenness, selfishness, discrimination and intolerance.

Together we can make our world a better place to live in and we start doing this in the home. Some of us only speak to children when we have to correct or scold them. Have good conversations with the young ones. They depend on us to show them the right way in a loving environment.

To love is to live

To live is to love

Without love

Life is empty

Do these things and you

Love yourself and others

If we observe these maxims, think before we speak, watch what we say and know when to say it, in addition to adopting a loving healthy life style, we should live longer happier lives and be considered wise and easy to get along with.

The pursuit of a virtuous life
is the answer to
peaceful and harmonious living

I have profited from these 'reminders to myself' as I like to call them, as that's exactly what they are, by rereading them anytime I can. The reason is that we are prone to error and fall into unwise ways of thinking, or react in ways which are not in our best interest especially in spur of the moment situations. By reading these maxims and sharing them with others we help ourselves to remember that there is a wise, healthy and constructive way to live. Reprint them and put them up in appropriate places, in the home, in schools and in the work place. You have my permission.

Anthony Webster

February 9, 2007

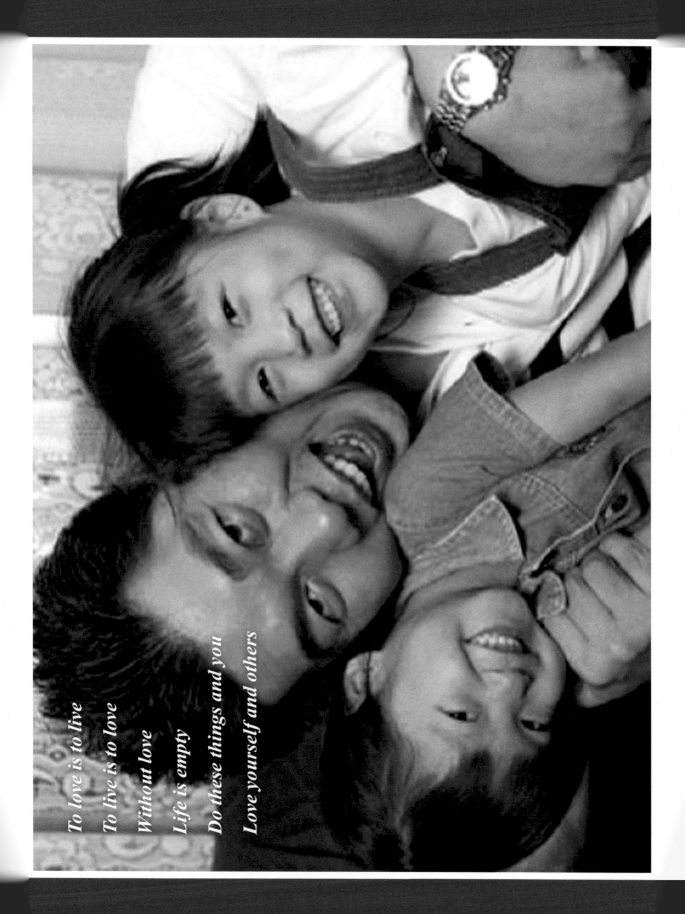

To love is to live
To live is to love
Without love
Life is empty
Do these things and you
Love yourself and others

CHAPTER 1

INTRODUCTION

How to love yourself and others

Man will never be able to unravel the mystery of life but at least we can try to appreciate it by valuing it and making the most of it. We are given the gift of life which consists of soul, mind and body by the Creator and placed on the planet to become real human beings—whole loving human beings.

This awareness should assist us to behave in a manner consistent with someone who has been given the awesome responsibility of taking care of such a wonderful gift. We do this first by loving and valuing ourselves. We love and value ourselves by following rules and principles which enable us to live a happy life—a life filled with purpose, caring, sincerity and serenity. There is nothing that can compare with such an achievement.

If you have seen the movies 'The Six Million Dollar Man' and' Robocop' you would realize that these are examples of the wonders of science in the quest to remake man or at least parts of him to enable man's body to function efficiently after an accident. They pale in comparison with the wonders of nature and the miracle of the human body. Here is one reason to love yourself; we are caretakers of the most magnificent and intricate piece of equipment created – the human body, which of course can only function if it has life, just as a vehicle can only function if it has a driver.

Get an education

Consider your soul (your life force) as the driver and your body as a priceless piece of equipment, loaned to you for your use and safekeeping for your life journey. Alas, some of us value and take greater care of our vehicles than of ourselves. Probably it's a good thing that human beings are not always taken up in how wonderful they are made as we may be tempted to stand around admiring ourselves all day.

I hope that I will be able to convince you that what matters most is that you take responsibility for these gifts seriously, enjoy them, take the best possible care of them and live in peaceful coexistent with others.

Chapter 2—The General Guidelines for Peaceful and Harmonious Living shows us how to love ourselves.

Chapters 3, 4 and 5 show us how to love our neighbours and keep out of trouble.

Appreciate life and value your worth

CHAPTER 2

GENERAL GUIDELINES FOR PEACEFUL AND HARMONIOUS LIVING

1. Respect authority

2. Get an education

3. Invest in Lifelong Learning (keep on learning all your life)

4. Accept responsibility for your life and your actions

5. Develop your talents

6. Use your initiative

7. Practice self control

8. Enjoy your life

9. Help others

10. Be considerate

11. Show appreciation

12. Try to live by the highest principles

Be a team player

CHAPTER 3

IDEALS AND PRINCIPLES FOR PEACEFUL AND HARMONIOUS LIVING AT HOME

1. Respect your parents

2. Don't waste time

3. Don't use other people's property without asking

4. Put things back after using them

5. Help around the house without being asked

6. Keep a clean scene

7. Attend to allocated chores

8. Find out / Ask before accusing

9. Discuss / Have conversations; don't argue

10. When you earn, contribute to the home

11. Train your children

12. Be disciplined (Get parents' permission first on key issues e.g. staying out late, giving away household items, inviting friends home, etc)

Obey road safety rules

CHAPTER 4

IDEALS AND PRINCIPLES FOR PEACEFUL AND HARMONIOUS LIVING IN THE OFFICE

1. Respect everyone

2. Don't Gossip

3. Organise / manage your time

4. Give an honest day's work for an honest day's pay

5. Look after the total well-being of employees

6. Support your boss

7. Be a team player

8. Keep learning

9. Have an open mind

10. Give your best to your organization / employer

We need to remind our children of the benefits to themselves of living virtuous lives.

CHAPTER 5

IDEAL AND PRINCIPLES FOR PEACEFUL AND HARMONIOUS LIVING IN PUBLIC

1. Respect everyone

2. Obey road safety rules

3. Be considerate

4. Give others a chance

5. Don't obstruct the pavement or the roadway

6. Greet others; return greetings

7. Don't interfere in other people's business

8. Help in any way you can

9. Think before you speak/act

10. Don't get into altercations; walk away (don't argue with an arguer)

11. Live and let live

12. Leave good enough alone(don't do things that will make matters worse).

Teach the children

EPILOGUE

I make no excuse for the brevity of this book for it is also written with the hope of getting those, who as a rule do not like or want to read, to read it. I have been encourage to make this book longer, but I resisted for two reasons, the one given above and the other: the hope that if you do not understand anything in it, that it would encourage 'good' talk, conversation, questions and discussion. If you have read from the beginning and reached this far I have achieved my first goal. If you have sought explanations or discussed anything contained within, I would have achieved my second goal.

This book will not be complete if I omit the words of the great teacher and exemplar of how to love—Jesus the Christ. The coming of Christ signalled a new dispensation. While the Ten Commandments will forever remain a guide to humanity of the rules of right conduct, Jesus reduced/summed up these commandments to two.

1. Thou shalt love the Lord thy God with thy whole heart, thy whole soul, thy whole mind and thy whole strength.

2. Thou shall love thy neighbour as thy self. This is not a book on religion, but it is a book about the second commandment loving yourself and your neighbour, which is the key to peace on the planet.

Finally remember that love is not just about a dry observation of these guidelines. Remember always that love comes from the heart and we need always to listen to our heart. Loving is about being observant to the need for love and affection in others and fulfilling them to the best of our ability.

To order—email: *lafgayl@live.com*

Printed in the United States
by Baker & Taylor Publisher Services